LIMERICKS
History, Humor, and How-To

Kevin DiBacco

New Castle Publishing

ISBN: 978-3-4627-1418-0 NEW CASTLE PUBLISHING

Dedication

To all who find joy in five lines,

where wisdom with humor

combines

Our Kevin, a masterful scribe

Made readers all part of his tribe

Each book that he wrote Got
everyone's vote

As laughter spread far and wide!

Table of Contents

The Amazing Journey of Limericks: A Fun Guide Through History

Have you ever caught yourself smiling at a clever five-line poem? You know the ones - they bounce along with that unmistakable rhythm and usually end with a witty punch line. Well, you're about to dive into the fascinating world of limericks, and trust me, their story is even more interesting than you might think!

INTRODUCTION

Let's Start With the Basics: What Makes a Limerick Tick?

Before we time-travel through history, let's crack open the hood and see what makes these poetic little machines run. A limerick is like a perfectly crafted joke in verse form - five lines of rhythmic genius that follow a specific pattern.

Think of it like a musical sandwich:
Two long lines at the top (the first slice of bread)

Two shorter lines in the middle (the filling)
One long line at the end (the bottom slice)

And they all dance to that unmistakable "da-da-DUM, da-da-DUM" rhythm. Here's a classic example to show you what I mean:

There once was a girl from the coast,
Who loved making cinnamon toast. She
baked all day long, Sang many a song,
Till her kitchen was filled with each
post!

Notice how those lines practically sing themselves? That's the magic of anapestic meter - fancy words for that bouncy rhythm that makes limericks so catchy and fun to recite.

The Surprising Origins: Not Just Bar Room Entertainment!

Now, here's where it gets interesting. Most people think limericks were born in pubs (and we'll get to that part of the story), but would you believe their earliest ancestors were actually written by monks? That's right - those medieval manuscript-copying masters would sometimes slip little five-line Latin verses into their work. Talk about hiding jokes in plain sight!

Picture this: It's the 1200s, and while most monks are carefully copying religious texts, some clever souls are sneaking in these little verses that follow a similar pattern to what we now know as limericks.

Here's a modern English version of what these early Porto-limericks might have been like:

A scribe in his cell late at night, Found his ink had turned watery and light. He mixed it anew, Added wine to the brew, And his words came out wonky but bright!

The Irish Connection: Why "Limerick"?

Now, here's where our story takes an interesting turn. You're probably wondering, "Why are they called limericks anyway?" Well, grab a virtual seat in an 18th-century Irish pub in the city of Limerick, and I'll tell you the tale. Limerick was a bustling port city where sailors, traders, and locals would gather in taverns after long days of work.

These pubs became creative hotspots - imagine a sort of medieval poetry slam, where people would compete to create the cleverest verses, they could. The winner often won a free pint, which might explain why so many people got so good at it!
What made these verses special was their unique mix of languages. You might hear:

English from the traders
Irish Gaelic from the locals

Sailor's slang from the seafarers

Even bits of French from visiting merchants

It was like a linguistic cocktail, and everyone was invited to take a sip!

Here's a modern limerick capturing that multicultural pub atmosphere:

In a Limerick pub long ago, Sat sailors with tales to bestow. In English and Irish, Their verses grew stylish, As pints made their creativity flow!

The Victorian Game-Changer: Enter Edward Lear

Now, let's zip forward to the 1800s, when something remarkable happened. Enter Edward Lear, a fascinating character who would completely transform the limerick's reputation. Imagine a slightly eccentric artist who:

Made his living painting parrots
Gave drawing lessons to Queen Victoria
Suffered from depression and epilepsy
Had a deep love of nonsense verse
In 1846, Lear published "A Book of Nonsense," and it changed everything. He took this pub entertainment and turned it into something entirely new - family-friendly verses paired with quirky illustrations. It was like taking street graffiti and turning it into a children's book (in the best possible way).

Here's one of Lear's most famous limericks:

*There was an Old Man with a beard,
Who said, "It is just as I feared! Two
Owls and a Hen, Four Larks and a
Wren, Have all built their nests in my
beard!"*

What made Lear's limericks special was:
They often featured impossible situations
The main character was usually introduced as "an Old Man" or "a Young Lady"
The last line often repeated the first line with a slight variation

Each came with its own silly illustration

The Global Takeover: Limericks Conquer the World

Thanks to the British Empire (and let's be honest, their habit of showing up uninvited around the globe), limericks spread worldwide faster than you could say "There once was..." They became like the first viral memes, adapting to local cultures and languages everywhere they went.

In India, they incorporated local flavors:

A raja who lived in Bombay Ate curry three times every day. When asked, "Isn't that hot?" He replied, "No, it's not! It's how we keep monsoons at bay!"

In Australia, they went bush:

A kangaroo hopping outback Kept joey safe in her pack. Through desert and plain, Through sunshine and rain, They followed the old wallaby track.

The Modern Era: Limericks Go Digital

Fast forward to today, and limericks are everywhere! They've jumped from pub walls to Twitter walls, from handwritten notes to TikTok quotes. They're being:

Generated by AI

Shared on social media

Used in advertising campaigns

Taught in classrooms

Written by corporate teams

Here's a tech-savvy limerick for you:

An influencer's latest TikTok Went viral and caused quite a shock. Her limerick dance Made millions advance, Till algorithms crashed from the block!

Why Limericks Are Perfect for Learning

Teachers love limericks, and for good reason. They're like the Swiss Army knife of educational tools:

For Language Learning:

They teach rhythm and rhyme

They help with pronunciation

They make vocabulary memorable

They're short enough to memorize

For Math and Science:

The squares of the first numbers show A pattern that helps students grow: One, four, then nine, sixteen - See what these digits mean? Math concepts in verse help them flow

For History: *When Columbus sailed over the sea In fourteen-ninety-two to be free, Three ships in his fleet Made history complete, Though his navigation was wrong, you'll agree!*

The Psychology of Why They Work

Ever wonder why limericks stick in your head like that catchy song you can't shake? It's all about how our brains work:

The rhythm matches natural speech patterns

The rhyme scheme is predictable but not boring

Five lines is the perfect length for memory

Humor helps information stick

The structure provides a satisfying closure

Writing Your Own Limericks: A Friendly Guide

Ready to try your hand at limerick writing? Here's your starter kit:

First Line Magic:

"There once was..." is always a safe start

Name a person and place

Make sure it ends with a rhyming word

Second Line Strategy:

Build on your character or situation

Keep the same rhythm

Rhyme with line one

The Short Line Pair:

Make them snappy

Keep them related

Make them rhyme with each other

The Big Finish:

Deliver your punch line

Rhyme with lines 1 and 2

Make it surprising or funny

Here's a template to get you started:

There once was a [person] from [place],

Who [did something time/space]. [Short

action or fact], [Related impact],

[Surprising result or grace].

Limericks in the Wild:

Modern Applications

Today, limericks are working harder than ever. You'll find them:

In Business:
Marketing campaigns
Training materials
Team-building exercises
Company newsletters
In Education:
Language classes
Science demonstrations
History lessons
Writing workshops
In Social Media:
Twitter challenges
Instagram captions
TikTok trends
YouTube content

The Future of Limericks

As we rocket into the digital age, limericks keep finding new ways to stay relevant. They're being:

Created by artificial intelligence

Performed in virtual reality

Shared across social platforms

Used in digital storytelling

Incorporated into apps and games

Why Limericks Will Never Die

The secret to the limerick's survival is its perfect balance of:

Structure and creativity

Simplicity and sophistication

Humor and wisdom

Tradition and innovation

The Never-Ending Story

From medieval monasteries to modern smartphones, limericks have survived because they tap into something fundamentally human - our love of patterns, our appreciation of wit, and our need to share stories and laughs with others.

Let's end with a meta-limerick about their journey:

From monasteries, taverns, and more,
Through centuries washing ashore,
These five-line delights Still brighten our
nights, And they'll live on for eons
galore!

Whether you're a limerick lover, a curious newcomer, or somewhere in between, remember: these five-line wonders have been making people smile for hundreds of years, and they're not going anywhere soon. So why not try writing one yourself? After all, there's always room for one more limerick in the world!

Chapter 1: The Journey

The limerick's journey through history is as fascinating as the form itself. From Irish pubs to Victorian parlors, from medieval taverns to modern classrooms, these five-line verses have evolved while maintaining their essential character.

Historical Timeline Examples:

Medieval Origins: There once was a medieval scribe Who wrote what the monks would prescribe His quill dipped

in ink Made letters that link Till stories
flowed forth from his tribe

Renaissance Period: A painter in
Florence did say That art should make
work seem like play With colors so bright
And perspectives right His canvas brought
night into day

Industrial Age: When steam engines first
came to be A worker exclaimed with great
glee "These pistons and gears Will change
coming years!" The future was destined to
see

Irish Heritage: A tavern in Limerick
town Where verses brought patrons
renown Each song and each tale Served
up with good ale Put smiles where there
once was a frown

The form evolved through various cultural
contexts:

Sailor's Tales: An old salt who sailed on the sea Told stories of what used to be Of mermaids and whales And thunderous gales While shipmates all listened with glee

Military Marches: The soldiers who marched off to war Found rhythm in verses they saw The cadence kept time As words made to rhyme Gave strength when their spirits were raw

Chapter 2: Anatomy of a Limerick

Basic Structure Explained: A limerick's architecture is precise, like a well-crafted piece of music. Each element serves a specific purpose in creating the perfect rhythm and flow.

Structure Examples:

Perfect Rhythm: If rhythm's the heart of your verse Make certain each line is well-versed The syllables flow Like waves to and fro Till patterns are clearly rehearsed

Line Length: The longer lines carry the tale While shorter ones never should fail To quicken the pace With rhythmical grace As story flows forward like sail

Key Elements Illustrated:

1. **First Line Setup: The opening sets up your scene Establishing what you might mean It catches the ear Makes listeners near**

And draws them in ways unforeseen

2. **Second Line Development:** The second line builds on the first Adding detail that might be dispersed It carries along The heart of the song Till plot points are properly versed

3. **Short Lines (Third and Fourth):** The middle lines quicken the pace Like runners who speed up their race They build to the end As storylines bend Toward finish with timing and grace

4. **Final Line Resolution:** The last line must tie it all up Like filling a half-empty cup It brings to an end The tale you did send While giving your readers a sup

Rhyme Scheme Demonstrations:

Perfect AABBA: The rhyming must follow its way (a) Through patterns of verse every day (a) The middle pair short (b) Give matching report (b) Then back to first rhyme we must stray (a

Advanced Techniques:

Internal Rhyme: A fellow who loved rhyming words Made verses fly free just like birds His internal chimes Rang multiple times Till echoes of rhyming occurred

Alliteration Added: Proudly prancing papers proceed Past paragraphs properly freed With wonderful words Like whispering birds Till trembling tongues take the lead

Multiple Meter Examples:

Strict Anapestic: In strictest anapestic time The verses must dance as they climb

Through da-da-DUM beat Make rhythm complete Till meter and meaning sublime

Iambic Variation: Some verses move soft then move strong Like gentle waves rolling along Their rhythmical way Through night into day Till weakness and power belong

Chapter 3: Types of Limericks

Classical Nonsense: There was an old duck in a pond Of swimming he grew rather fond He practiced all day In his waterly way Till ripples would magically bond

More Nonsense Examples:

*A curious creature named Blip Would
dance on the edge of a ship With
tentacles ten He'd spin now and then Till
sailors would give him the slip*

*A puzzling beast from the zoo Had spots
that were purple and blue It sneezed
glitter dust When winds gave a gust And
sparkled the whole evening through*

Historical Limericks:

Ancient Times: *When Caesar crossed
over the Nile The crocodiles watched
with a smile His boat slightly leaked
While servants all peeked At reptiles
stretched out single file*

Renaissance: *Da Vinci while sketching
one day Found wings that might help
people play His drawings took flight*

Through dreams in the night Till flying machines found their way

Modern Era: When Edison lit up the night The people all gasped at the sight Electric displays Turned darkness to days And changed how we lived with new light

Geographic Variations:

European: *A gondola floating in Rome Made tourists feel quite far from home Through canals they'd glide While guides stepped inside To show them where angels would roam*

Asian: *On mountains in old Japanese prints The snow leaves such delicate hints Of pathways that wind Leave footsteps behind While cherry trees scatter their tints*

American: *The Grand Canyon stretches so wide With colors that cannot hide The layers of stone Stand proudly alone While rivers cut paths deep inside*

Chapter 4: Writing Classic Limericks

Essential Elements:

Character Introduction: A character needs to be clear When first in your verse they appear Their traits should shine through In just words a few Till readers feel they're standing near

Setting the Scene: The setting must quickly take hold Whether warm places or cold A few words suffice To paint paradise Or dungeons both dank and old

Building Tension: The tension must build line by line Like grapes being turned into wine Each moment gets strong As verse moves along Till meaning turns water to wine

Resolution: Resolution brings sweet release Like signing a treaty of peace The end must feel right Bring closure to light And let all the tension-strings cease

Chapter 5: Famous Limerick Writers

Edward Lear's Style: There once was a master of rhyme Who wrote silly verses sublime His nonsense would flow Like rivers below Till children loved reading each time

More Lear Examples:

There lived an Old Man in a tree Who danced with a bird and a bee They twirled round and round Till falling they found The ground wasn't where it should be

Lewis Carroll's Mathematical Mind: A logician lost in his thoughts Tied reasoning up into knots Through paradox deep His mind tried to leap Till logic lay scattered in spots

Chapter 6: Modern Interpretations

Contemporary Style: *A blogger who lived on their phone Made digital verse all their own Through hashtags and tweets Their limerick fleets Went viral and widely were known*

Technology Themes: *A coder debugging their app Found errors that caused quite a trap The semicolon missed Made functions resist Till coffee restored mental snap.*

Social Media: *An influencer seeking their fame Through TikTok and Instagram came Their content would flow As followers grow Till algorithms knew their name.*

Chapter 7: Seasonal and Holiday Limericks

Through the Calendar:

Winter Wonderland: *When snowflakes first dance in the air They blanket the world without care Each crystal unique Makes patterns that speak Of winter's sophisticated flair*

More Winter Examples:

The skater who glided on ice Found movements precise and so nice She twirled and she spun Till daylight was done And moonlight made silver suffice

A snowman stood guard in the yard His carrot nose frozen quite hard With coal for his eyes He watched winter skies And served as a frosty regard.

Spring Awakening:

Cherry Blossoms: *In springtime when blossoms take flight They paint all the*

*morning in white Each petal that falls
Like nature that calls Makes poetry
bloom in the light*

Garden Growth: *A gardener planting in
spring Found seeds were a marvelous
thing They sprouted with care In warm
morning air Till flowers made happiness
sing.*

Summer Scenes:

Beach Days: *The waves on a
midsummer shore Keep rhythm with
ocean's deep roar While children at play
Make castles all day Till tide washes
tracks from the floor*

Picnic Time: *A picnic spread out on the lawn From midday straight through until dawn With treats wrapped in gold And stories untold Till fireflies led evening on*

Autumn Glory:

Harvest Moon: *September's bright harvest moon glows While autumn winds gently dispose Of leaves red and gold Both young and quite old Till winter's first crystalline snows*

Halloween: *A jack-o'-lantern's bright grin Lights pathways where children begin Their trick-or-treat quest All costumed and blessed With candy stored safe in their bin*

Holiday Specials:

Christmas Eve: When stockings are hung with great care And cookie scents fill evening air The children all sleep While Santa's deer leap Across rooftops everywhere

New Year's Eve: As midnight approaches with haste Not moments are left there to waste The old year retires As new year aspires To memories yet to be traced

Valentine's Day: A valentine sealed with a kiss Brought feelings of pure lovers' bliss The heart-shaped delight Made everything right Till romance could hardly miss

Chapter 8: Educational Limericks

Mathematics:

Addition Fun: *The numbers lined up in a row Had places they needed to go Add units with care Then tens they declare Till sums make the answers to show*

Multiplication: *Times tables are fun to recall When rhythm helps numbers not fall Like seven times eight Makes fifty-six great And patterns help memorize all*

Division Skills: *Division brings sharing to life When numbers cut clean as a knife The quotient appears As remainder clears And fractions resolve without strife*

Science Lessons:

Solar System: *The planets spin round and round While gravity keeps them all bound From Mercury near To Neptune so far In orbits both stable and sound*

States of Matter: *A molecule floating in space Can change both its form and its face As solid it's still As liquid will spill As gas fills available space*

Biology: *The cell is a factory small With parts that respond to each call The* *nucleus guides While membrane*

provides Protection surrounding it all

Grammar and Language:

Parts of Speech: *The nouns and the verbs in a line Need adjectives help them to shine While adverbs explain How actions maintain Their meaning in ways that define*

Punctuation: *A comma knows just where to pause Like taking a breath without cause It separates clear Makes meaning appear Following grammatical laws*

Chapter 9: Professional Limericks

Medical Field:

*A doctor who worked through the night
Found ways to make everything right
With stethoscope near And patients to
cheer Till wellness returned with
daylight*

Legal World:

*A lawyer who studied each case Found
evidence leaving its trace Through
documents long Both right and quite
wrong Till justice found proper embrace*

Teaching Profession:

A teacher who loved every class Helped knowledge and wisdom to pass Through lessons well planned Each mind would expand Till learning became unsurpassed

Chapter 10: Advanced Limerick Techniques

Double Entendre:

A fisher who cast in the rain Found catching two meanings was plain His line and his words Like schools of bright birds Both captured more than he'd explain

Complex Wordplay:

A punster composed with delight Made meanings both wrong and quite right His write and his right Caused readers to write "Right writing makes writing right, right?"

Nested Narratives:

A story within stories told Of heroes both timid and bold Each tale interweaves Like autumn's crisp leaves Till patterns of plot would unfold

Extended Metaphors:

Life's garden needs tending with care

Like verses that float through the air

Each seed that we plant Like words that

we grant Grows meanings for others to

share

Chapter 11: Modern Themes

Digital Age:

A coder who lived in the cloud Of virtual

spaces was proud Through bits and

through bytes Through days and

through nights Their programs made

algorithms crowd

Social Media Life:

*An influencer's daily routine Meant
posting each moment they'd glean
Through filters and frames Playing
social games Till viral their content was
seen*

Remote Work:

*A worker who Zoomed through their day
Found cats would quite often display
Their tails and their fur Would cause
quite a stir While meetings would
meander away*

Artificial Intelligence:

*A chatbot that learned how to sing Made
verses with digital spring Though
technically sound Something profound*

Was missing from each mechanical thing

Chapter 12: Future of the Form

Evolution:

The limerick continues to grow As new ways of sharing will flow Through screens yet unknown And formats unshown Till future forms no one can know

Virtual Reality:

In spaces of virtual light Where poetry takes digital flight Each verse that we share Through electronic air Makes traditional boundaries slight

Interactive Verse:

*Tomorrow's bright verses will change As
readers and writers arrange New
patterns to flow New rhythms to grow
Till limerick forms rearrange*

Final Thoughts:

*The beauty of five lines remains Though
methods of sharing sustain New changes
each day As time makes its way The
limerick's charm will maintain*

Experimental Forms:

*A hologram floating in space Showed
limericks changing their pace Through
dimensions three For all folks to see Till
reality bent with such grace*

Chapter 13: Regional Variations of Limericks

British Style:

From London's old cobblestone streets
Come verses with rhythmical beats The
cockney rhyme slang Makes meanings
that rang Till humor with wordplay
completes

A Yorkshire man speaking his mind Left
proper pronunciation behind His dialect
strong Made verses belong To regions of
particular kind

Irish Traditional:

From Dublin to Kerry's green shore The limericks flow evermore With wit sharp and clean And meanings between The lines that tradition holds store

The pub life in Limerick town Still keeps ancient verses' renown Through music and tale And good Irish ale The stories pass endlessly down

Scottish Highlands:

Among highland heather and hills Where bagpipes make musical trills The verses flow free Like streams to the sea With brogue that the atmosphere fills

American Regional:

New England: A yankee from old Boston town Wore verses like dignified crown

His proper speech ways Through cold winter days Made formal words earn their renown

Southern Style: *A Georgian's sweet summer verse Flowed slow as molasses disperse Each drawling word said Like honey fresh spread Made hurrying seem quite perverse*

Midwest Flavor: *The prairies stretch endless and wide Where verses flow in with the tide Of wheat fields that sway Through long summer's day While stories spread far countryside*

Australian Outback:

*A stockman who rode in the heat Found
verses made journeys complete Through
bush and through scrub Past billabong's
hub Till stories made circles complete*

Caribbean Rhythm:

*Island verses dance on the breeze
Through palm trees that sway in the seas
Each tropical rhyme Keeps Caribbean
time Till poetry flows with such ease*

Asian Influences:

*A verse from the old Shanghai way
Combined Eastern thoughts of the day
With limerick form Till new styles were
born And East met with West in
wordplay*

Japanese Fusion: *Like haiku but
longer in kind These verses leave silence*

behind Five lines to express What

seventeen stress In patterns that please

Eastern mind

Chapter 14: Limerick Games and Teaching Tools

Classroom Challenges:

Word Chain Game: *Begin with a limerick to start Then next player must take their part Using last word to lead To next verse indeed Till chain grows to show verbal art*

Example Chain: *There once was a cat with a hat Who danced on a colorful mat*

The mat was so bright It shone in the night Till morning showed where the cat sat

Next player must use 'sat': A princess who gracefully sat On throne made of silk, just like that The cushion beneath Made sitting a wreath Of comfort fit more for a cat

Teaching Tools:

Fill-in-the-Blank: There once was a _____ from _____ Who loved to _____ and to _____ One day they _____ Which made people _____ And that's why they _____ today

Vocabulary Builder: Each week brings a new word to learn Through verses that help students earn Their meaning through rhyme One word at a time Till language skills they can discern

Example: The word "perpendicular" stands At right angles, just as commands From floor straight to wall Ninety degrees all Till geometry all understand

Interactive Games:

Round Robin: The classroom sits round in a ring Each adding one line while they sing Five students in turn Make verses to learn Till limerick circles take wing

Speed Challenge: With timer set down to the wire Quick verses spark creative fire Just two minutes spent Till rhyming is bent Into shapes that young minds inspire

Team Competitions:

Verse Volleyball: Two teams trading verses with speed Each matching the rhythm indeed Back forth goes the rhyme In measured quick time Till winning team takes verbal lead

Theme Tournaments: The classes compete through the year With themed verses round after round From seasons to space Each team sets its pace Till championship time draws near

Learning Assessment:

Grammar Check: Identify parts of each line Where nouns and where verbs intertwine Mark adjectives clear See adverbs appear Till parts of speech students define

Rhythm Practice: Now tap out the beats as they flow DA-da-da, DA-da-da, just so The shorter lines too Have rhythm run through Till patterns help learning to grow

Memory Tools:

Historical Dates: In fourteen-ninety-two they say Columbus sailed water's wide way Three ships in his fleet Made history sweet Till New World was found on that day

Scientific Facts: The planets in order align From Sun outward, each in design From Mercury's heat Past Jupiter's feet Till Pluto got cut from the line

Chapter 15: Occupational Limericks Expanded

Medical Professionals:

The Surgeon: *A surgeon with hands calm and sure Performed operations so pure Each cut with great care Made healing repair Till wellness could fully secure*

The Nurse: *A nurse working late through the night Kept watch till the dawn's early light With comfort and care They're always right there Making everything turn out all right*

The Pediatrician: *A doctor who worked just with kids Made checkups like fun on the skids With jokes and with smiles And playful-styled trials Till fear of the doctor forbids*

Technology Sector:

The Programmer: *A coder who typed through the night Made algorithms work just right Through loops and through strings Through digital things Till bugs had all taken their flight*

The IT Support: *Support desk received quite a call "My computer won't work at all!" "Have you tried to see If plugged it might be?" The solution was rather small*

The Data Scientist: *With data spread out on their screen They searched for the patterns between Each number displayed Till trends were portrayed And insights could clearly be seen*

Education Field:

The Math Teacher: *A teacher of algebra found That numbers would dance all around Through equations long Like verses in song Till solutions were finally found*

The Art Instructor: *An artist who taught with such flair Made colors dance high in the air With brushstrokes so bold New visions unfold Till creativity bloomed everywhere*

The Gym Coach: *A coach with a whistle of gold Made exercise never grow old Through jumping and play Each physical way Built strength in the young and the bold*

Legal Profession:

The Judge: *A judge sitting high on their bench Made justice not flinch or not clench Each case that they heard Got* *wisdom-filled word Till fairness no fact could entrench*

The Defense Lawyer: *A lawyer defending their case Found evidence leaving its trace Through details so small That might save it all Till truth found its rightful place*

The Prosecutor: *A state lawyer building their proof Kept justice beneath every roof With facts lined up neat Made arguments sweet Till truth stood completely aloof*

Trades and Crafts:

The Carpenter: *A woodworker skilled with their tools Made furniture following* *rules Each joint fit so tight Each finish so bright Till masterwork broke all the rules*

The Plumber: *A plumber who worked underground Fixed pipes making thunderous sound The water sprayed high Nearly touched the sky Till problems were fixed, safe and sound*

The Electrician: *An expert in currents that flow Made power run high and run low Through circuits complete Made systems so neat Till darkness had nowhere to go*

Service Industry:

The Chef: *A chef in a five-star cuisine Made dishes none ever had seen With spices rare And flavors to share Till dining became quite supreme*

The Barista: *A coffee artist supreme Made beverages flow like a dream Each cappuccino A work of casino Till customers burst with esteem*

The Flight Attendant: *Above clouds so fluffy and white An attendant made everything right Through turbulent air They served with such flair Till landing completed the flight*

Chapter 16: Nature and Environment

Ecosystems:

The Rainforest: Deep *in the rainforest green Where wonders have never been seen The canopy high Touches tropical sky While mysteries flourish between*

The Desert: *A desert stretched endless and dry Where sand dunes reach up to the sky The scorpions creep While temperatures keep The hardiest creatures nearby*

The Arctic: *In landscapes of crystalline white Where auroras dance in the night*

The polar bears roam Through ice-covered foam Till summer brings endless daylight

Climate Change:

Rising Tides: *The oceans are rising each year As glaciers just disappear The shorelines recede While scientists heed The warnings that nature makes clear*

Changing Weather: *The patterns of weather have changed As seasons get quite rearranged With winters too warm And summers that storm Till normal seems quite out of range*

Hope for Future: *Young voices are rising today To keep climate change held at bay Through actions quite bold Both young and the old Unite to find Earth-saving way*

Wildlife:

The Endangered: *A tiger whose numbers decline Through forests grows harder to find Protection must come Before they succumb To fate that leaves none of their kind*

Conservation: *The rangers who guard nature's space Keep poachers from leaving their trace Through vigilant care And methods quite rare Help species maintain their own place*

Recovery: *A species once thought to be lost Returned from the edge of all cost Through breeding programs And habitat balms Till numbers no longer were crossed*

Natural Cycles:

Water Cycle: *A raindrop that fell from above Joined rivers that endlessly move Through streams to the sea Then clouds to be free Till cycles eternally prove*

Carbon Cycle: *The carbon moves round and around Through air, sea, and deep in the ground Plants breathe it right in While animals win As balance in nature is found*

Nitrogen Flow: *The nitrogen fixed in the soil Through bacteria's diligent toil Helps plants as they grow While cycles still flow In patterns that nothing can spoil*

Seasonal Changes:

Spring Awakening: *When winter ice starts to retreat And springtime makes entrance so sweet The buds start to show As warm breezes blow Till nature's revival's complete*

Summer's Peak: *The longest of days in the year When sun makes its power appear The flowers all bloom No sign of gloom Till autumn starts drawing quite near*

Autumn's Turn: *September brings changes so bold As leaves turn to crimson and gold Each tree in its time Makes colors sublime Till winter takes seasonal hold*

Natural Wonders:

Grand Canyon: *The river carved deep through the stone For millions of years all alone Each layer revealed What time had concealed Till history's pages were shown*

Great Barrier Reef: *Beneath azure tropical seas The coral sways soft in the breeze With fish darting through In waters so blue While nature works hard to appease*

Chapter 17: Sports and Recreation

Ball Sports:

Baseball: *A pitcher who stood on the mound Made fastballs spin round and* *around The batter stood there With focused-fixed stare Till strike three made victory sound*

Basketball: *A player who danced with the ball Made moves that seemed not real at all Through defenders tight With skills taking flight Till scoring made stadium walls fall*

Soccer/Football: *A striker who curved through the field Made defenders practically yield The goal in their sight Shot taken just right Till victory finally sealed*

Olympic Sports:

Gymnastics: *A gymnast who flew through the air With grace that was far beyond rare Each flip and each turn*

*Made audience learn What beauty in
motion could share*

Swimming: *A swimmer who cut through
the pool Made ripples break every rule
Each stroke smooth and clean Through
water unseen Till records fell, precious
as jewel*

Track and Field: *A sprinter coiled ready
to spring When starter's gun made ears
ring Down straightaway flew Like wind
as it blew Till finish line made victory
sing*

Leisure Activities:

Golf: *A golfer addressing the tee Saw
hazards where hazards could be The
swing smooth and slow Made little ball*

go Till hole nineteen's drinks set them free

Fishing: *An angler who rose before light Found peace in the pre-dawn's delight The cast and the wait For fish to take bait Made morning seem perfectly right*

Hiking: *A hiker who climbed to the peak Found views that made tired legs weak The trail had been long But spirit stayed strong Till summit made everything speak*

Team Sports:

Hockey: *On ice slick as glass they would glide With puck flying side unto side The checks and the shots Made fans lose their thoughts Till overtime winners decide*

Rugby: *The scrum pushed with might and with main Through mud and through wind and through rain The ball squirted free For all fans to see Till try-line brought victory's gain*

Volleyball: *Above net stretched high in the gym They leaped with both power and vim Each spike and each save Made audiences rave Till match point made everything trim*

Extreme Sports:

Skateboarding: *A skater who rode through the park Made tricks look as light as a lark Each flip and each grind Left gravity blind Till darkness brought end to their arc*

Rock Climbing: *A climber who scaled sheerest wall Found handholds though they were quite small Each move planned with care Through thin mountain air Till summit prevented all fall*

Surfing: *A surfer who rode morning waves Found peace that their spirit still craves Through pipeline's curl Where waters unfurl Till evening light finally saves*

Chapter 18: Science and Technology

Computer Science: *A programmer coding all night Found bugs that just wouldn't work right Through loops and through strings Through all kinds of things Till dawn brought the fix into sight*

Space: *An astronaut floating in space Observed Earth with infinite grace Through windows that showed How oceans all glowed While stars kept eternal embrace.*

Medical Science: *A doctor examining cells Found stories each microscope tells Through patterns so small That might* *save us all While research all mystery dispels*

Chapter 19: World Cultures and Traditions

Cultural Festivals: *At Diwali's festival bright The lamps set the darkness alight With colors so bold And stories of old Till morning ends magical night*

Traditional Customs: *A Japanese tea ceremony Flows graceful as waves in the sea Each movement precise Like patterns in ice Till harmony sets spirits free*

Folk Tales: *A storyteller's tales of yore Kept audiences asking for more Through legends sublime Through riddles in rhyme Till wisdom filled evening's bright store*

Chapter 20: Food and Cuisine

Cooking Adventures: *A chef with experimental flair Mixed flavors with passionate care New recipes tried As tastes multiplied Till critics all praised with fanfare*

Regional Specialties: *A pasta made fresh in Rome Made travelers feel right at home The sauce rich and red The wine flowing spread Till evening bade no one to roam*

Chapter 21: Transportation and Travel

Aviation: *A pilot who soared through the cloud Of flying was naturally proud Through storms they would sail Through thunder and hail Till landing made passengers crowd*

Maritime Adventures: *A sailor who crossed seven seas Found stories in each ocean breeze Through waves mountain high Through storm-darkened sky Till harbor brought welcome release*

Chapter 22: Arts and Entertainment

Theater: *An actor on opening night Gave Shakespeare new meaning and might Each line crystal clear Made audience cheer Till curtain call brought pure delight*

Dance: *A dancer who spun through the air Moved graceful beyond all compare Each leap and each turn Made watchers all learn How beauty brings moments so rare*

Chapter 23: Architecture and Design

Famous Buildings: *The Eiffel Tower piercing sky Makes visitors wonder just why Its intricate frame Brought Paris such fame Till centuries still pass it by*

Urban Planning: *A city planner's grand design Made streets and parks perfectly align With spaces for all Both large and quite small Till community spirit could shine*

Chapter 24: Economics and Business

Market Trends: *An investor watching the trace Of markets move up at swift pace Through charts that revealed What futures might yield Till profits found perfect embrace*

Entrepreneurship: *A startup that grew from one room Found success like flowers in bloom Through hard work and skill Through strong force of will Till fortune replaced former gloom*

Chapter 25: Philosophy and Thought

Ancient Wisdom: *A philosopher pondering deep Found questions that wouldn't let sleep Through logic's clear light Through darkness of night Till wisdom made ignorance weep*

Modern Dilemmas: *The questions of modern-day life Bring answers with digital strife Through screens that we hold Through networks that fold till truth cuts like wisdom's sharp knife*

Chapter 26: Weather and Climate

Seasonal Changes: *A meteorologist's chart Shows patterns that set days apart Through sunshine and rain Through weather's domain Till forecasts become nature's art*

Extreme Weather: *A hurricane's powerful might Brings wind through the* *darkness of night Through rain-laden sky Through clouds racing by Till morning brings new day's clear light*

Chapter 27: Fashion and Style

Historical Fashion: *A Victorian lady's fine dress Made onlookers stop and confess Such elegant style Made fashion worthwhile Till trends set new standards to bless*

Modern Trends: *A designer's latest creation Brought forth much anticipation Through runway display Through fashion's array Till style met with great acclamation*

Close

"History, Humor, and How-To" provides a comprehensive look at the enduring poetic form of the limerick. The book explores the limerick's origins in 18th century Ireland as an oral tradition used for pub songs, social commentary and memory aids. It traces the limerick's evolution through the Victorian era, when Edward Lear popularized it as a written form of family-friendly humor, up to modern times where it serves purposes ranging from education to creative expression to social commentary.

The book looks into the anatomy and writing craft behind a limerick's five lines, AABBA rhyme scheme, and anapestic rhythm. It showcases different types of limericks, from the nonsensical and whimsical to the satirical and thought-provoking. Famous limerick writers like Edward Lear and Lewis Carroll are profiled, while a variety of examples demonstrate the form's versatility in capturing different time periods, regional dialects, and cultural contexts throughout history.

For the modern writer, the book provides a wealth of ideas and inspiration for using limericks today. In the classroom, limericks can make learning subjects like math, science, grammar and vocabulary more engaging and memorable. As a creative writing exercise, limericks offer endless opportunities for wordplay, storytelling, character and scene development. Limericks can add wit and levity to professional settings like medical, legal, and tech workplaces. The book shows how the limerick form can be adapted to reflect current events and themes, from life in the digital age to artificial intelligence to social and environmental issues.

Looking ahead, the book envisions how limericks will continue to evolve and stay relevant in the future. Interactive digital formats and technologies like virtual reality may create new ways to experience and experiment with limericks. However, the core characteristics that have helped limericks endure for centuries will remain constant. At its heart, the limerick will always be a clever, concise way to share a moment of humor and insight that delights both writer and reader.

Here is a final recap limerick that captures the book's key themes:

This guide shows how wit and wisdom hold fast Through five lines that rhyme the form stands the test of time as future verse echoes the last!

Index

A

B

W